POSTCARD HISTORY SERIES

The Lafayettes

This postcard is a greeting from Lafayette, Indiana. The front reads: "Well! here I am, in / La Fayette, Ind. / Enjoying its sights and cheer, / Everything's great and I'm feeling first rate, / But oh! how I wish you were here." It was copyrighted in 1908 by O.E. Hasselman and mailed in 1910. (Author's collection.)

ON THE FRONT COVER: This postcard shows a crowd of football fans at the Purdue-Wisconsin game on October 17, 1914. The contest was held in Wisconsin, and the Badgers beat the Boilermakers 14-7, which is written on the card. Purdue ended the season with a 5-2 record. One of the ladies in the crowd is wearing a "W" on her sleeve. (Author's collection.)

ON THE BACK COVER: This postcard shows Main Street in downtown Lafayette in the 1950s. Rexall Drugs is no longer there, along with many other stores. The card was published by Harvey's Studio in Lebanon, Indiana. (Author's collection.)

POSTCARD HISTORY SERIES

The Lafayettes

W.C. Madden

ARCADIA PUBLISHING

Copyright © 2018 by W.C. Madden
ISBN 978-1-4671-2848-3

Published by Arcadia Publishing
Charleston, South Carolina

Printed in the United States of America

Library of Congress Control Number: 2017953966

For all general information contact Arcadia Publishing at:
Telephone 843-853-2070
Fax 843-853-0044
E-mail sales@arcadiapublishing.com
For customer service and orders:
Toll-Free 1-888-313-2665

Visit us on the Internet at www.arcadiapublishing.com

Contents

ACKNOWLEDGMENTS

I would like to thank the Tippecanoe Historical Association for the use of its facility to research some of the information for this book. Thanks to several departments at Purdue University for providing information.

I owe gratitude to the sellers of these postcards. Thanks to Penrod/Hiawatha for allowing me to use some of their postcards for the book. Thanks to Cardcow.com for carrying many postcards that I purchased. Also, thanks to the collectors who sold me their postcards on ebay.com.

I'd also like to thank my wife, Janice, for lending me assistance in the preparation of this book. She's been my favorite reader, editor, and cheerleader ever since I began writing books.

Unless otherwise noted, images used in this work come from the author's collection.

INTRODUCTION

This book is titled *The Lafayettes* because most of the postcards come from the cities of Lafayette and West Lafayette, Indiana. Some also come from the nearby town of Battle Ground.

Lafayette was rich in French heritage long before it was named after the famed French general Marquis de Lafayette. French fur traders came to the area in the early 1700s. France claimed the area and called it New France. The government of New France established a military outpost, Fort Ouiatenon, to protect against Great Britain's western expansion. The outpost was established along the Wabash River in 1717 and was taken over by the British in 1761. A couple of years later, on June 1, 1763, a group of braves simply walked in and took Lt. Edward Jenkins and his few men as prisoners. After the French and Indian War, the British abandoned the fort. Americans secured Fort Ouiatenon in 1778, but local tribes took it over in the 1780s and used it as a base of operations in their resistance against the westward expansion of white American settlers. Pres. George Washington ordered the fort destroyed in 1791. A force led by Col. John Hardin chased away the Indians and burned the fort to the ground.

A replica of Fort Ouiatenon was built in 1930 near where the fort was located by local physician Richard Wetherill, one of the founders of the Tippecanoe Historical Association. However, the replica blockhouse does not match the style or type of construction of the original fort, which was much larger. Recently, the true location of the old fort was discovered. Every fall, a reenactment of pioneer life in the days of the old fort is held at the park near the replica fort; it is called the Feast of the Hunter's Moon.

In 1824, William Digby purchased land on the banks of the Wabash and hired a surveyor to plat his holdings. A year later, he named it Lafayette after the famous general, who had toured Indiana that year. The following year, Tippecanoe County was created, and Lafayette became the county seat.

The town became known as a river city, because most transportation to and from it was by the Wabash River. The population increased until it became large enough to be a city in 1853.

By the time postcards came about in the late 1800s, Lafayette was becoming one of the major cities in Indiana; it had a population of 18,116 in 1900.

Some of those early postcards showed a city that was thriving, with tall buildings being erected downtown, various bridges being thrown across the Wabash River to neighboring West Lafayette, churches thriving, and new schools being built.

Lafayette continued to grow, and the population increased to about 40,000 by the 1960s. From the 1960s to the 1990s, the population remained flat, but the city began to annex more area, and growth began to occur again as major industries settled in the community.

Nowadays, Lafayette has grown to more than 70,000 inhabitants, according to estimates by the US Census Bureau.

Growth across the Wabash River from Lafayette was slow at first, as three small villages popped up: Chauncey, Oakwood, and Kingston. Kingston was laid out in 1855 by Jesse B. Lutz. Chauncey was platted in 1860 by the Chauncey family of Philadelphia. Chauncey and Kingston formed a municipal government in 1866 and selected Chauncey as the town's name.

In 1869, Lafayette businessman John Purdue offered $150,000 for a university in Tippecanoe County, and the Indiana General Assembly established Purdue University. Classes began at Purdue on September 16, 1874, with six instructors and 39 students. The university began to grow along with the community.

In May 1888, Chauncey voted to change its name to West Lafayette. By then, the growth of the university was fueling the growth of the little town.

By February 1889, Purdue University had grown to an enrollment of 430 students. The following year revealed a population of 1,242 in the city.

For many years into the 20th century, Purdue University was given a Lafayette address, which is why many of the early postcards were identified that way. However, West Lafayette has now developed into a thriving community with a big-city government.

West Lafayette and Purdue University have collaboratively built an innovative, knowledge-based local economy that is evolving and expanding. In 1961, the Purdue Research Park was established. It has become home to more than 100 high-tech companies with 2,500 employees and offers state-of-the-art communications infrastructure, world-class research facilities, a business incubation complex to help start-up firms, and scenic walking trails and lakes.

Today, the enrollment of Purdue University exceeds 40,000 per semester, with an academic staff of more than 3,000. The population of the city has grown to an estimated 45,000.

Also within West Lafayette is the Indiana Veterans' Home, which was called the Indiana State Soldiers' Home at first. It was created in 1895, when the Indiana General Assembly unanimously passed a bill to create it and appropriated $75,000 for its buildings. The state purchased 187 acres from Tippecanoe County, and the City of West Lafayette gave an additional 55 acres to the home. The county also donated $5,632.50 in cash to the effort. A local veteran and businessman, Gen. Richard P. DeHart, gifted a 1,900-foot strip of riverfront property to the home as well. Today, this land is known as the Tecumseh Trails Park.

Contracts were awarded on July 8, 1895, and work began on seven buildings. The home first opened on February 1, 1896, and was formally dedicated on July 4. Additional funds were appropriated in 1897, and the Old Men's Home and a chapel were built. By 1900, the home had nine state buildings, five cottages, a public restaurant, a commandant's residence, a surgeon's cottage, and a carpentry and paint shop.

Battle Ground is situated just north of West Lafayette and is a popular place for visitors because of its historic battlefield. The Battle of Tippecanoe was fought at this location on the morning of November 7, 1811. Gen. William Henry Harrison with his army of 1,000 men had arrived at the location the day before and camped there overnight. They were supposed to meet with the Shawnee Prophet, but he chose to attack the camp in the middle of the night. The Americans lost 63 men in the battle. The army burned down the nearby Indian village in retaliation and disbursed the Indian nation that Tecumseh had tried to organize.

Harrison returned to the site of the battle to give speeches during his first presidential campaign in 1835.

The battlefield began attracting visitors and picnickers in the 1850s. A refreshing artesian spring was discovered there. Then the Louisville, New Albany & Salem Railroad laid its tracks along the eastern edge of the site. A large wooden-frame refreshment stand was erected on the land adjacent to the battlefield to serve the growing number of visitors.

In 1873, the battle site was enclosed by an iron fence. The Methodists developed a campground just to the north. In 1908, the state erected an 85-foot marble obelisk on the site for $24,500 to honor those who died in the battle. By the early 1920s, the campground had become a youth retreat area.

On October 9, 1960, Tippecanoe Battlefield was named a national historic landmark. The following year, a crowd estimated at 10,000 attended the 150th anniversary of the battle.

However, in the following years, the site became less trafficked and fell into disrepair. The Tippecanoe County Historical Association restored the site and now maintains it and the seminary building, which houses a museum related to the battle. An amphitheater was added to the memorial in 1986.

Various events and festivals are held on the grounds today, and it is a popular place for visitors once again.

One

LAFAYETTE

This postcard of the Marquis de Lafayette is likely from about a hundred years ago. The city of Lafayette is named for the famous Frenchman who fought in the American Revolutionary War. He was made a major general during the war and served with distinction in the Battle of Rhode Island. The postcard was produced from his portrait in Mount Vernon. The artist is unknown.

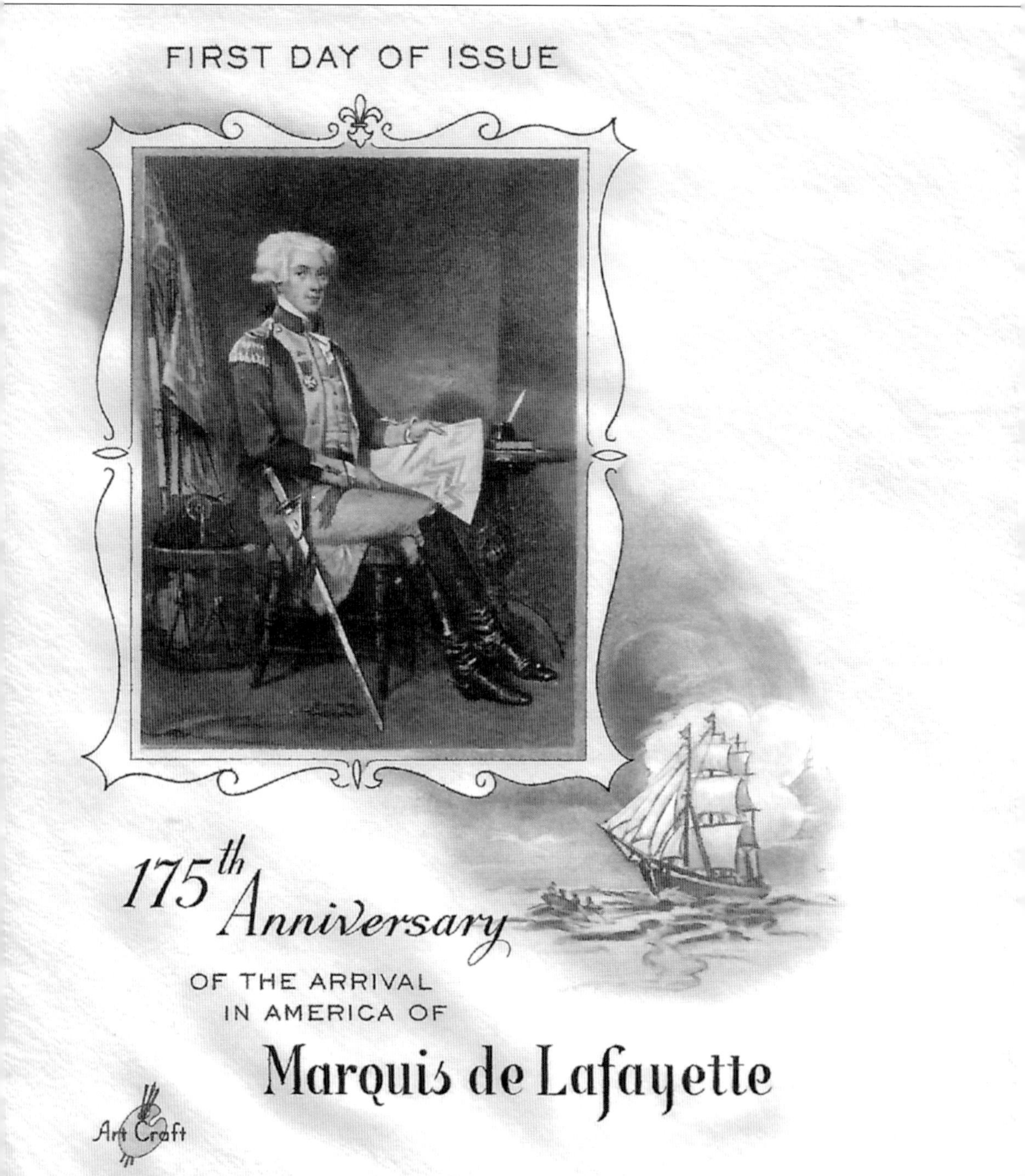

This envelope and stamp mark the 175th anniversary of the arrival in America of the Marquis de Lafayette. It was stamped in Georgetown, South Carolina, on June 13, 1952. Lafayette was sometimes known as the "Hero of the Two Worlds." He arrived in this country at North Island on Winyah Bay, South Carolina, on June 13, 1777. His first battle was at Brandywine on September

11, 1777. After the battle, Gen. George Washington cited him for bravery. He stood alongside Washington at Valley Forge in the winter of 1777–1778 and shared the hardships of the weather with his troops. The famed general toured Indiana in the 1830s.

The Tippecanoe County Courthouse was constructed of Indiana limestone between 1881 and 1884. The courthouse has 100 columns and nine statues. It went through a thorough cleaning in 2012 to make it shine. It was not so shiny when this postcard was produced, probably in the 1940s. Lady Liberty stands atop the elongated dome.

This postcard shows the Tippecanoe County Courthouse in 1976, when the US bicentennial was held. A man tried to bomb the courthouse on August 2, 1998, by driving a bomb-laden pickup truck through the east doors of the courthouse. Since then, security has been much tighter.

This postcard shows the east side of the public square in Lafayette around the beginning of the 20th century. No cars are shown, but there is an electric streetcar on Fourth Street. A law office was in the corner building. This postcard was mailed in 1909.

An electric railcar zooms past the Tippecanoe County Courthouse in this scene of Main Street west of Fourth Street in the early 1900s. The Lafayette Street Railway was electrified in 1888, and railcars were used up until 1940, when they were replaced by buses. This postcard was mailed in 1914.

This postcard shows Main Street west of Fourth Street in downtown Lafayette. The Lafayette County Courthouse is on the left. Railway tracks ran up and down Main Street as well as Fourth Street at the time. Most of the buildings on the right are still standing today, but a few farther down Main Street have been replaced by taller high-rises.

This postcard was likely published around the turn of the 20th century, based on the attire of the people depicted. The sender wrote that he went to Battle Ground. It was sent to someone in Jeffersonville, Indiana. The publisher of the postcard is unknown.

This postcard shows people drinking out of the fountain below the statue of General Lafayette. The fountain was erected in 1887 by the City of Lafayette. It contains a number of details about the history of the general, courthouses, city founder, and other information on its eight-sided base. The drinking fountain was converted to a display fountain some time ago.

Mrs. W.F. Reynolds donated this old house to the Lafayette Public Library in 1901. The library had previously been in the Lafayette High School building. The Reynolds home was on a large piece of ground encompassing an entire city block at Fifth and South Streets. It remained there until 1927. The first public library opened in 1882.

The Albert A. Wells Memorial Library, made possible by a gift of $100,000 from Dr. Wells, was opened to the public in 1927. At the time of this postcard, likely produced in the 1930s, the library contained about 60,000 volumes. It served as the Tippecanoe County Library until a new one was built in 1989. Now the building serves as the Wells Community Cultural Center.

This 1950s postcard shows that Main Street was a bustling thoroughfare at the time. Rexall Drugs is no longer there today. The street is not as busy these days, because shoppers have options in other parts of the city. This postcard was produced by Harvey's Studio.

Construction began on the Knights of Columbus Pythian Home in 1926, and the building was dedicated on August 10, 1927. The home began as an orphanage. In 1942, it was turned into a retirement home for members. Later, it became a nursing home for the public. It met its demise in the 1990s and was sold to the Lafayette School Corporation in 1992. It was later torn down.

The Cary Home for Children was created through a donation by Frank M. Cary in 1929. The home was named in memory of his wife and dedicated on November 31, 1930. Until 1972, the home operated as an orphanage. It later became a treatment center for adolescent boys and is still a treatment center today. This postcard was probably created soon after it was completed.

This postcard, which was mailed in 1949, shows the former Elks clubhouse in Lafayette. Elks Lodge 143 was originally in this building on the northeast corner of Fifth and South Streets. The Elks held their last meeting here on September 17, 1966. Everything was then moved to a country club. The building was razed in 1967.

The Lafayette Loan and Trust occupied this building 100 years ago. The bank began in 1893. Bank mergers have since occurred, and the bank became the Lafayette Bank & Trust, which merged with First Merchants Bank in 2001. This building at Fourth and Main Streets has been altered, and First Source Bank took over the space in 2010. This postcard was mailed in 1917.

The Lafayette Life Insurance Company was founded in 1905 and had this building erected at 300 Main Street in 1919. The company's headquarters have since moved to Cincinnati. A Wabash Valley Trust plaque was awarded to the Neoclassical building in 1990. The Community Foundation of Lafayette now occupies the building along with a law firm and other businesses.

This was the office building and general headquarters for the Brotherhood of Painters, Decorators, and Paperhangers of America. It was erected in 1920–1921 at an approximate cost of $175,000 and was dedicated on January 25, 1922. The brotherhood has since moved to a building on South Thirtieth Street in Lafayette.

Masonic Lodge No. 123 was founded in 1852 in Lafayette. The lodge was called the Lincoln Club and met in this building until 1967. Then the lodge moved into a building at 522 Columbia Street. The membership of the lodge is in excess of 100 and includes a mix of long-time and newer members of a variety of ages.

The YMCA constructed this building at the corner of Seventh and Columbia Streets in downtown Lafayette. Ground was broken on August 9, 1906, and the structure was dedicated on September 11, 1907. The final cost was $59,126.39, a hefty sum at the time. The YMCA has since moved to a new building on South Eighteenth Street.

The Lafayette Historical Association, which began in 1928, purchased the Moses Fowler House in 1940. This postcard shows the rear of the house. The 30-room Gothic Revival residence was built in the 1850s. The association built a new office complex next to the Moses Fowler House in 1977. The association sold the house in 2015 to the 1852 Foundation, which is trying to restore it.

The Wetherill Memorial Room was located in the Moses Fowler House. The room was named after Dr. Richard B. Wetherill, one of the founders and a president of the Tippecanoe Historical Association. He passed away in 1940. A large portrait of him hung over the fireplace mantel.

The Wabash Valley Sanitarium was built on the banks of the Wabash River, as printed on this postcard. The sanitarium opened in 1906 as a Seventh-Day Adventist institution. In 1969, after a merger, it became the Mental Health Center for Tippecanoe County. The sanitarium has since been demolished.

Nurses and doctors pose at the Wabash Valley Sanitarium in the early 1900s. The hospital was founded by Ellen G. White in 1906. It specialized in hydrotherapy and dietary regimens at first. It offered a three-year nursing course in the 1920s. In the 1930s, the emphasis was on nervous disorders.

St. Elizabeth Hospital, La Fayette, Ind.

St. Elizabeth Hospital in Lafayette was opened in 1876 by six members of the Sisters of St. Francis of Perpetual Adoration from Germany. It launched the St. Elizabeth School of Nursing in 1897. The hospital was at Fourteenth and Tippecanoe Streets. This postcard was mailed in 1909 from Lafayette to someone in Rushville, Indiana.

Bird's-eye View of St. Elizabeth Hospital, Lafayette, Indiana

By 1929, when this postcard was mailed, St. Elizabeth Hospital in Lafayette had become quite large, as seen in this aerial view. It became St. Elizabeth Central. In 2016, the hospital was renamed Franciscan Health Lafayette Central. It now has 155 beds for patients and provides many services.

The St. Francis Chapel at the hospital is at the southwest corner of the St. Elizabeth campus, nearest the corner of Tippecanoe and Fourteenth Streets. Masses are held daily and on holy days. It is always open to the public. This postcard was mailed in 1934.

This early postcard shows a six-horse team exhibited by J. Crouch & Sons of Lafayette. Crouch began importing horses in 1882, and by 1885, the company had established the Lafayette Stock Farm. The card says that the company was the largest importer in America of Percheron, Belgian, shire, German coach, and Hackney stallions and mares. One of Crouch's Belgian stallions won first prize at the 1904 St. Louis World's Fair.

The Cathedral of St. Mary of the Immaculate Conception was built on a hill on South Street in 1866, and celebrated its 150th anniversary in 2016. Today, it boasts a membership of about 1,000 families, according to church officials. This postcard was mailed to someone in Oakland, California.

This postcard shows St. Mary's Cathedral and its school. Today, the St. Mary's Cathedral School teaches preschoolers and grades one, two, and three. The school is the first step children take in the Lafayette Catholic school system. Kim Delaney was the principal of the school for the 2017–2018 school year.

This is what the inside of St. Mary's Cathedral looked like more than 100 years ago; it is quite different these days. The Roman Catholic church was led by Fr. Jeff Martin in 2017. This postcard was produced by Curteich of Chicago.

Trinity Methodist Church was constructed from 1869 to 1873 and was dedicated on March 23, 1873. The church was formally organized in 1827 and met in the old log courthouse. The basement was hand dug in 1933 by the Homebuilders Sunday school class. Numerous upgrades and remodeling have since been done. This postcard was mailed from Swindon, England, for three pence in 1959.

This postcard identifies this church as the Second Presbyterian Church. However, it was renamed the Central Presbyterian Church when the First and Second Presbyterian Churches combined in 1914. The church on North Seventh Street was built in 1895 but suffered a fire a year later. It was then rededicated in 1897. The spire was taken down sometime before 1921.

The First Baptist Church on North Seventh Street was dedicated on October 6, 1872. The church has traced its roots to 1835, when nine members joined together to form it. The early members met in various locations until the congregation built its first church in 1844 on the west side of Sixth Street and opened with a membership of 107.

The Wabash River begins in Ohio and runs west past Lafayette on its way to the Ohio River. The 529-mile river is the Ohio's largest tributary. It is the state river of Indiana and the subject of the state song "On the Banks of the Wabash, Far Away," by Paul Dresser. This postcard was mailed from Lafayette to someone in Alexandria, Indiana, in 1913.

This postcard says that this is the Little Wea Creek in Lafayette, but it actually shows the Wabash River. It may be where the creek flows into the Wabash. The creek is undoubtedly named for the Wea tribe, who once lived in the area of Lafayette. It is located west of the city.

The Main Street levee was located along the Wabash River by the Main Street Bridge. This postcard was mailed in 1952 to someone in Indianapolis. It was published by the Harry Kaplan News Agency and cost 2¢ to mail. The Wabash River was first mapped by French explorers.

This truss bridge at Main Street in Lafayette over the Wabash River to West Lafayette was built in 1890. Additional trusses were added by the Fort Wayne and Wabash Valley Traction Company in 1895. It was destroyed by flooding in 1913 and was replaced by another bridge in 1914.

This postcard shows cars traveling on the Main Street Bridge in Lafayette. This particular bridge was constructed in 1914. Lafayette converted the bridge to pedestrian use in 1993, and it was named in honor of John T. Myers, a US representative from 1966 to 1996.

The postcard above, titled "Birdseye View of La Fayette, Ind. and Wabash River," was made in Germany. The city is not actually visible in the postcard, but the Wabash River is in plain view. The Wabash turns south after it passes Lafayette, so the city may actually be in the background of this postcard. The postcard below shows Lafayette from a hill across from the Wabash River. The name comes from Ouabache, the spelling given by French traders for the Native American name for the river. The river's worst flood came in 1913.

This postcard shows the rocky ford of Wildcat Creek in Lafayette. It was mailed in 1907 to someone in Logansport. It was published by Pearson-Ullberg Company of Minneapolis. The north fork of Wildcat Creek runs from Kokomo to Lafayette before emptying into the Wabash River. It also has a south fork that runs to Dayton.

This postcard shows three fishermen on the Tippecanoe River. The card says that the river is near Lafayette. In fact, the Tippecanoe River is a couple miles east of Lafayette and flows into the Wabash River. The river flows past the city of Monticello on its way to the Wabash.

The back of this postcard states that the Columbian Park Recreational Center was a place for the promotion of American ideals for educational, cultural, and athletic activities. It had a seating capacity of 3,500 and was donated by Bert and June Loeb. It was dedicated in 1940. The field was renamed the Bert E. Loeb Stadium in 1971 and became the home of the Colt World Series.

Columbian Park was created in 1893 and was named after the World's Columbian Exposition, held in Chicago that same year. Before then, the area was known as Lafayette Park and Reservoir Park. It is the largest park in Lafayette and has many walking paths as well as shelters for picnics and the Columbian Park Zoo. This postcard was mailed from Lafayette to someone in Otterbein on May 21, 1908.

The postcard above has two mistakes: it spells the park as Columbia instead of Columbian and spells Lafayette as La Fayette, which was a common spelling of the city in its early days. The lake now contains Memorial Island, named to honor veterans of Lafayette and serve as a permanent reminder of the price paid for freedom. Below is another view of the lake in Columbian Park in the early 1900s. Someone is pictured on the walking bridge over the lake. This postcard was mailed to someone in Lafayette in 1912. It was published by the M.G. Callahan Company of Germany and Marion, Indiana.

Columbian Park has had animals for patrons to view for a long time. In the early 1900s, the park had these two buffaloes; this postcard was mailed in 1917. The Columbian Park Zoo is the second oldest zoo in the state and was founded in 1907. Today, the zoo has many more animals than it did in the early days.

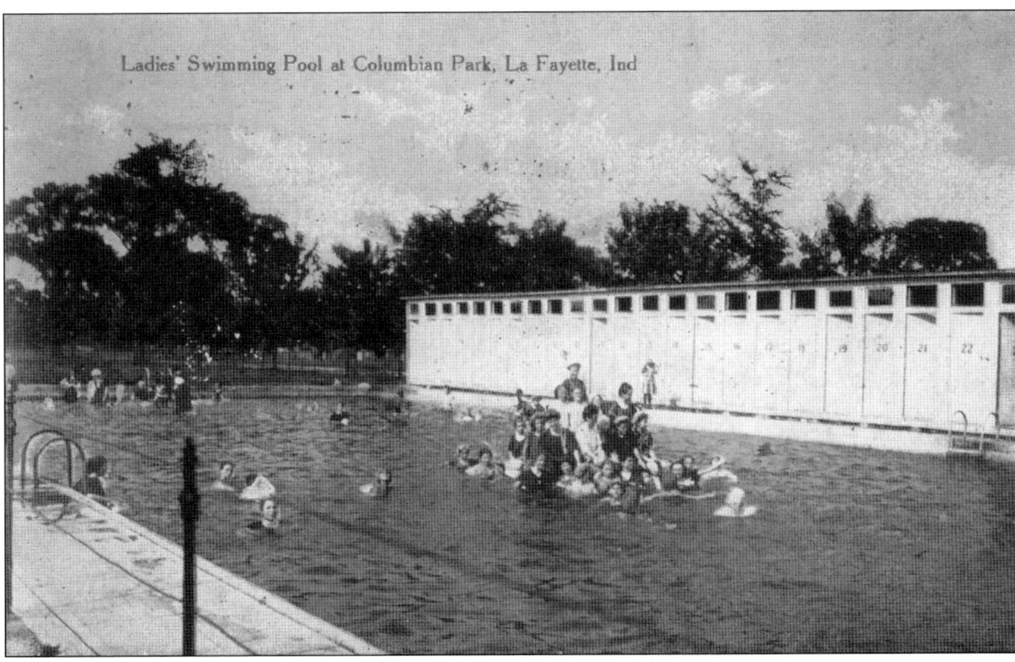

In the early 1900s, women had their own swimming pool, according to this postcard that identifies the Ladies Swimming Pool at Columbian Park. Today, the park boasts a large pool called Tropicanoe Cove. The city has several other pools as well. This postcard was mailed in 1911.

This 1950s postcard shows a round pool at Columbian Park. That pool has since been replaced by Tropicanoe Cove, which has the spiraling Banana Peel tube slide to Cattail Crik. The pool is open from Memorial Day until Labor Day, and a season pass costs $100.

This colorful postcard depicts Main Street at night in "La Fayette." Although the city was never spelled this way, many early postcards had Lafayette as two words, and in French it is sometimes spelled as two words. The postcard was mailed from West Lafayette in 1908 to someone in Nora, Indiana.

In 1873, public school authorities acquired a former township school at Kossuth and Dayton Roads. They then enlarged it and opened it as the Oakland School for elementary students. Citywide enrollment was reported as being about 6,000 students in 1873.

This was the Lafayette High School that opened in 1890. It replaced the first high school, which was opened in September 1864 in part of the old Central School building, with J.T. Merrill as its first principal. The publisher of the postcard is unknown.

The postcard above simply reads "High School," but its formal name was Jefferson High School. The school replaced the aging Lafayette High School at Sixth and Columbia Streets. The new school, named after Pres. Thomas Jefferson, was erected between Ninth, Tenth, Elizabeth, and Cincinnati Streets. It opened its doors in January 1912 and was dedicated on April 2. The school was in operation in this building until 1970, then it served as a Tippecanoe Junior High School. It later became the home of Ivy Tech Community College and New Community School. The old school is now apartments for the elderly. The postcard below is from a photograph of the school probably taken in the 1950s and was published by Harvey's Studio.

Washington Elementary School first opened in 1901 at the corner of Eleventh and Elizabeth Streets. It was dedicated on February 22, 1901. The school closed in 2006. It last served children from kindergarten through the fifth grade. In 2017, there were nine elementary schools in Lafayette.

This postcard shows the entrance to Greenbush Cemetery in the early 1900s. The cemetery is owned by the Greenbush Cemetery Association, first organized on February 12, 1848. Nearly 10,000 people are buried there, including the founder of Lafayette, William Digby. Also buried in the cemetery are soldiers from many wars, beginning with the Civil War.

The Lahr Hotel in Lafayette was at Fifth and Main Streets. Rooms in the early 1900s, when this postcard first appeared, were $1.50 and up. Built in 1848, it had 150 rooms, a café, and a cafeteria. It became famous when James A. Moon committed suicide here using a guillotine device on June 12, 1876. Today, it is an apartment complex.

The Hotel Fowler was an Arthur L. Roberts hotel with 200 fireproof and air-conditioned rooms, the Blue Blazer Cocktail Lounge, and the Walnut Room Café. This postcard was postmarked in 1954 and sent from Lafayette to someone in Adrian, Michigan. The building is now the Fowler Apartments and is owned by Cypress Realty.

The Combs Motor Court was on Schuyler Avenue in the 1950s, when this postcard was produced. It had 18 deluxe units, but the motor court went out of business like many old motels and motor inns of that era. They have been replaced by more modern options.

The Devon Plaza Motel was on US 52 in the 1950s, when this postcard was printed. The motel is still thriving today, but many motels have died out and been replaced by larger hotel chains in the Lafayette area, such as Holiday Inn, Best Western, and Days Inn.

The original Holiday Inn of Lafayette used to be at the intersection of US 52 and Indiana State Road 26, according to this postcard that was provided to guests in the 1970s. That hotel closed and was replaced by two other Holiday Inns in the city. One is now located by Interstate 65, and the other is downtown on South Street.

The Green Acres Motel was built along US 52 North in Lafayette. The back of this postcard says that the motel had 20 modern cottages with 10 deluxe units, a playground, and a restaurant nearby. It was three miles north of Purdue University and was approved by the American Automobile Association.

The Sarge Biltz restaurant was opened by Charles W. "Sarge" Biltz at the intersection of Indiana Highways 24 and 52 at the edge of Lafayette in the 1930s. It grew quickly into one of the state's most famed eateries and was a popular rendezvous for people attending athletic events at Purdue University.

The Flame restaurant was on the Indiana 52 Bypass in Lafayette in the 1960s. It had two floors of dining and was open on Sundays. It also had the Prime Rib Room for banquets. This postcard was mailed in 1970. The company had other locations in the state.

The Romanesque-style New York Central Depot, also known as "Big Four Depot," was built in Lafayette in 1902. This was its original location before it was moved to Second Street. The move was a huge operation that occurred over four days, September 14–17, 1994. It was then rededicated as the centerpiece of the James F. Riehle Plaza.

The Traction Line, an electric streetcar railway, ran from Lafayette to the Wabash Valley Sanitarium on the south side of the Wabash River from 1896 until it was abandoned on October 31, 1930. The sanitarium was three miles from downtown Lafayette. It served as a quiet retreat for the tired businessman and offered hydrotherapy.

The last Monon Depot used in Lafayette was built in 1960, after the depot downtown was discontinued in 1959. The old depot downtown was converted into a theater for plays. The last Monon Depot, at Salem Street, was used until the Monon Railroad line quit running in 1971.

La Fayette, Ind., from the N. Y. Central Lines Bridge.

Downtown Lafayette can be seen in this postcard from the old New York Central Lines bridge that ran over the Wabash River from West Lafayette. The New York railroad began the Indianapolis, Lafayette & Cincinnati line in the late 1860s; it was extended to Chicago in 1873. The railroad was abandoned in early 1976. This postcard is dated 1908.

The Haan Mansion Museum was originally the State of Connecticut Building at the 1904 St. Louis World's Fair, as shown in this postcard postmarked 1904. The mansion was built with the intention of being dismantled and moved. It was moved by train to Lafayette to become the home of Mrs. And Mrs. William Potter. The Haan family purchased it in 1984 and turned it into a museum.

This was the Lafayette residence of James M. Fowler, president of the First National Bank of Fowler. The bank began in 1900 and closed in 1931. During its 32 years, it printed $231,480 worth of national currency. The bank was located in Benton County and was assigned charter No. 5,430.

National Homes Corporation of Lafayette produced these types of homes when it was in business. This was its Thrift model and was sold at the lowest cost. Homes of these types were built all over the United States. The company was incorporated in 1940 and built prefabricated and modular homes, apartments, mobile classroom units, and mobile homes.

This postcard shows Sixth Street looking north in the early 1900s. It was postmarked in 1908 and sent to someone in Indianapolis. Sixth Street was tree lined and had curbs and streetlights. At the far end of the street is a horse and wagon, but it is barely visible.

The Central Fire Station, also known as Station No. 1, was built in 1910. It had two poles for firemen to slide down to get to their fire trucks. It was in service until 1965 and was torn down a couple of years later. As of 2017, Lafayette had seven fire stations, a training center, and an administrative center.

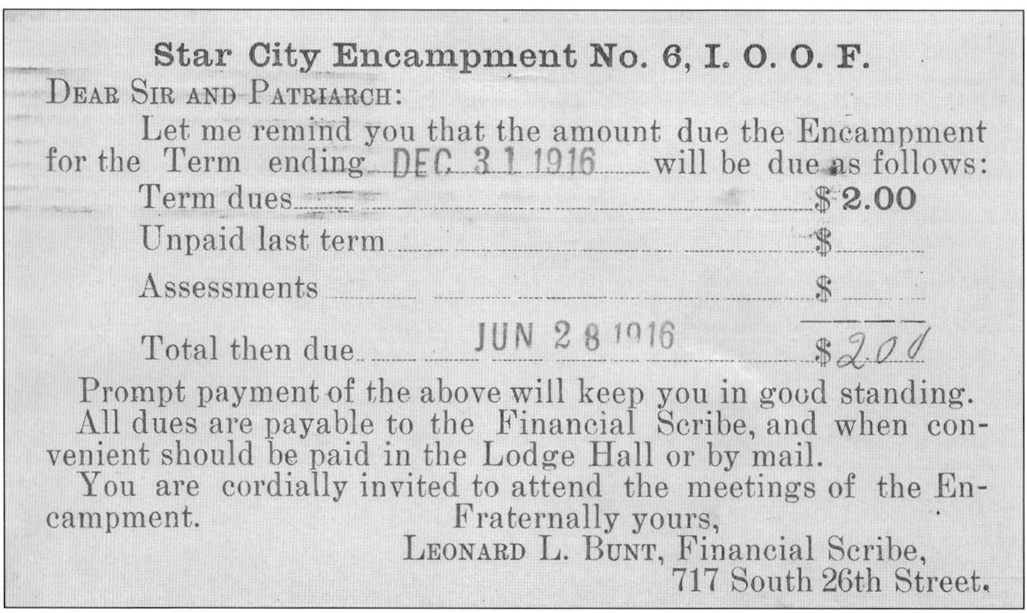

Star City Encampment No. 6, I. O. O. F.

Dear Sir and Patriarch:

Let me remind you that the amount due the Encampment for the Term ending DEC 31 1916 will be due as follows:

Term dues .... $ 2.00

Unpaid last term .... $

Assessments .... $

Total then due ..... JUN 28 1916 ..... $2.00

Prompt payment of the above will keep you in good standing.

All dues are payable to the Financial Scribe, and when convenient should be paid in the Lodge Hall or by mail.

You are cordially invited to attend the meetings of the Encampment.

Fraternally yours,
Leonard L. Bunt, Financial Scribe,
717 South 26th Street.

It was not uncommon to use postcards to send bills, and the practice continues today with some companies because of the cost of postage. This particular card was from Star City Encampment No. 6, International Order of Odd Fellows. The organization mailed this bill for dues from Lafayette in 1916.

William Digby was the founder of Lafayette in 1824. The following year, he decided to name the town after the famous French general, Marquis de Lafayette. This postcard comes from a painting of Digby. It was published in 1925.

William Digby, Founder of Lafayette, Ind. From painting by George Winter, 1852.

"The original Town of Lafayette was laid out May 25, 1825, by William Digby. Two days later he filed a copy of the original plat in the United States Land Office at Crawfordsville. He named the town after General de Lafayette, a French General, who aided this country in obtaining its independence."

This early postcard jokingly reads "I'm in a driving business," with a man driving a nail with a hammer. The novelty postcard was mailed from someone in Lafayette in 1906 to someone in Detroit, Michigan. It was made of leather like some early postcards until 1909, when the US Postal Service banned their use.

The Lafayette Music Conservatory began in 1904 with Lena M. Baer as president. The conservatory's goal was to hold four concerts a year, and most years it held more than that. The conservatory lasted until 1943, when it died out. At first it was located on North Fourth Street, and then moved to Columbia Street.

This postcard of the Lafayette Country Club may have been created soon after it first opened in 1909. The private club on South Ninth Street is still active today with a nine-hole golf course, a swimming pool, tennis courts, a fitness facility, and first-class dining facilities.

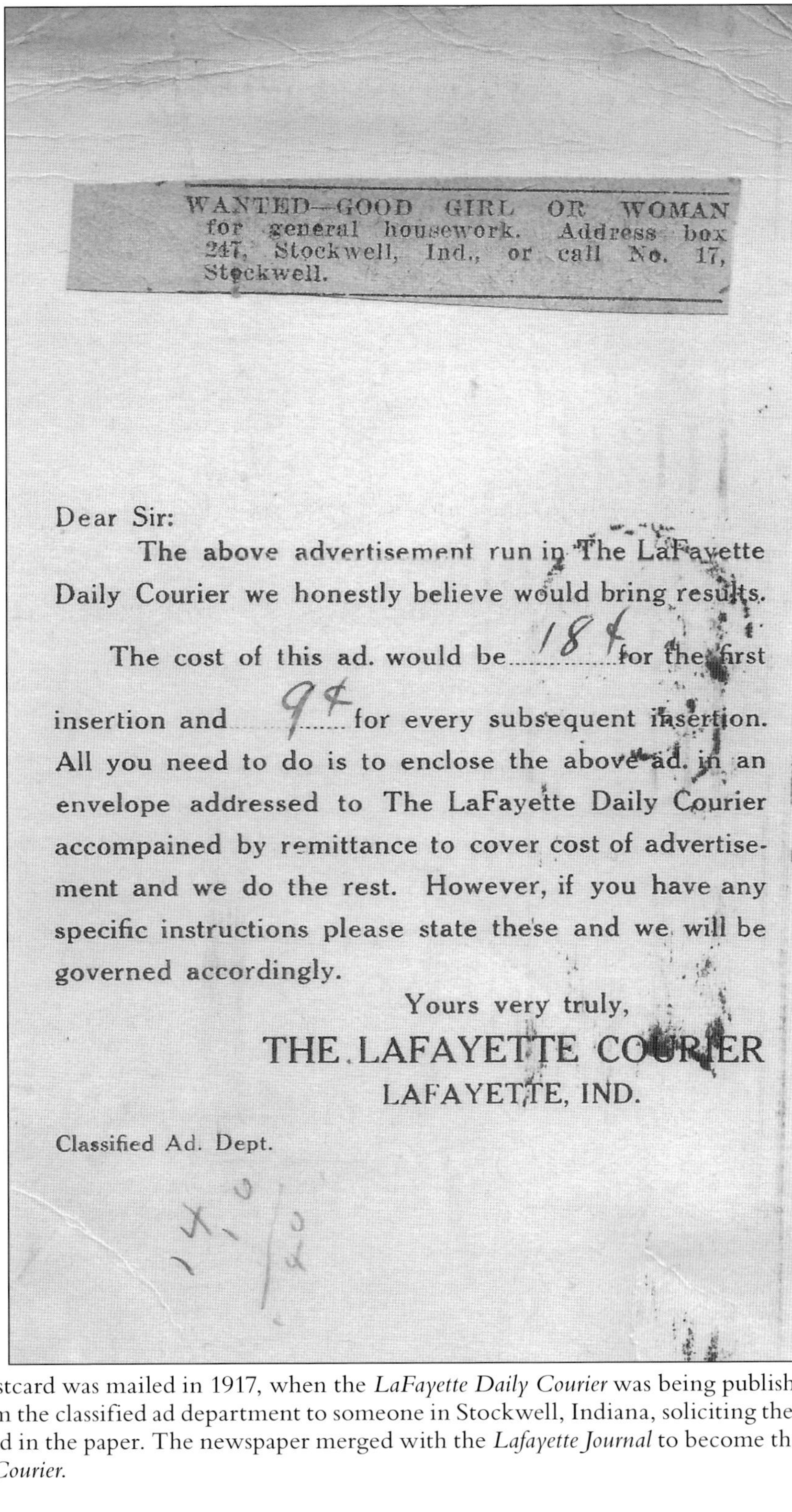

WANTED—GOOD GIRL OR WOMAN for general housework. Address box 247, Stockwell, Ind., or call No. 17, Stockwell.

Dear Sir:

The above advertisement run in The LaFayette Daily Courier we honestly believe would bring results.

The cost of this ad. would be 18¢ for the first insertion and 9¢ for every subsequent insertion. All you need to do is to enclose the above ad. in an envelope addressed to The LaFayette Daily Courier accompained by remittance to cover cost of advertisement and we do the rest. However, if you have any specific instructions please state these and we will be governed accordingly.

Yours very truly,

THE LAFAYETTE COURIER
LAFAYETTE, IND.

Classified Ad. Dept.

This postcard was mailed in 1917, when the *LaFayette Daily Courier* was being published. It was sent from the classified ad department to someone in Stockwell, Indiana, soliciting the person to run an ad in the paper. The newspaper merged with the *Lafayette Journal* to become the *Lafayette Journal Courier.*

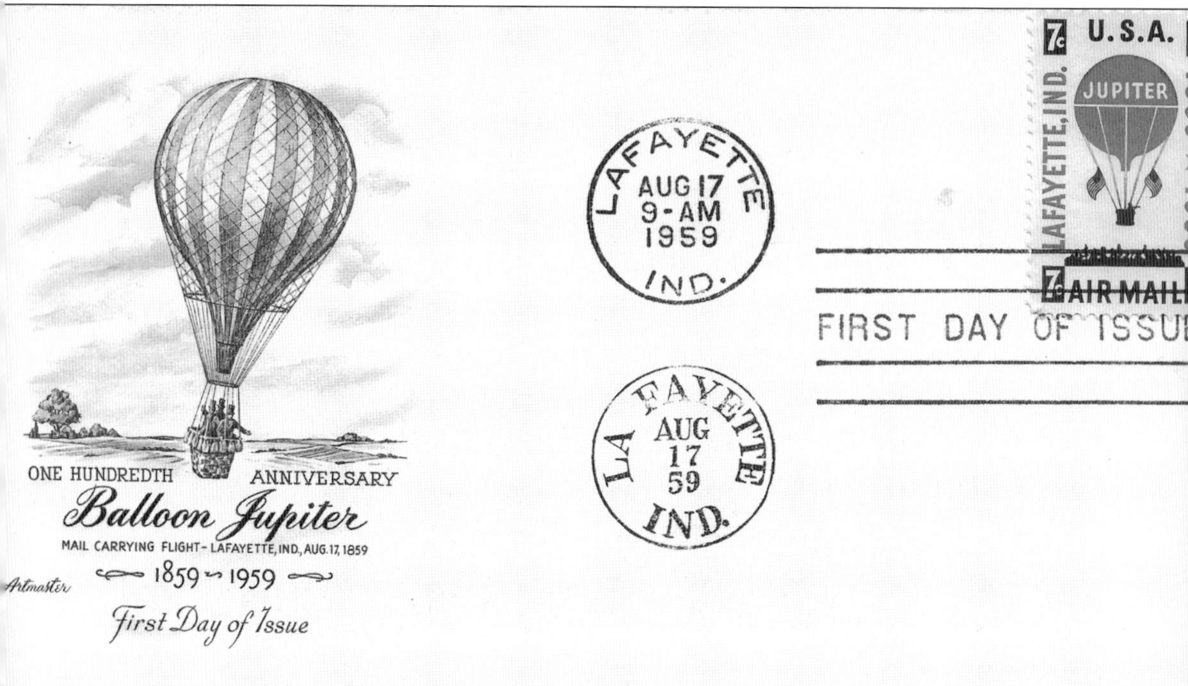

The US Postal Service issued a memorial letter on August 17, 1959, to commemorate the 100th anniversary of the balloon *Jupiter.* Although not a postcard, the letter is significant as it marks the anniversary of the first officially sanctioned airmail flight when John Wise attempted a "transcontinental voyage" from Lafayette to New York City.

This was the US Post Office in downtown Lafayette until it was replaced in 1932 with a new post office on Fourth Street. When it was first built is unknown. This postcard was postmarked in 1918 and sent to someone in Huntington, Indiana. Lafayette's first postmaster was Samuel Sargent in April 1826.

The present US Post Office downtown is in the Charles A. Halleck Federal Building on Fourth Street. It was constructed in 1930–1931. Halleck served in the US House of Representatives. This postcard was mailed in 1940 to someone in Randolph, Kansas. Today, Lafayette has five post office locations.

This postcard shows young girls riding horses. It is from the Sycamore Valley Girl Scout Camp on East State Road 26 in Lafayette. The camp boasts 160 acres of gently rolling meadows, Wildcat Creek, and forests just outside the city. It is still in use today.

In the early days of Lafayette, there were plenty of farms in the community, so haying occurred quite frequently. Today, there are not many farms within the borders of the city. When this card was mailed in 1909, Lafayette's population was only 18,116; it is now more than 70,000.

This postcard shows the cocktail lounge at Star Lanes when the bowling alley was new in the early 1950s. The bowling alley is still in use today at 1701 Schuyler Avenue, with 24 lanes. More than 30 people work there, and it has annual sales of more than $1.5 million.

This postcard was made in Germany and shows Lover's Lane along the Wabash River in Lafayette. The lane could well have been Tecumseh's Trail, which was actually in West Lafayette. Today there are few walking paths along the Wabash River in Lafayette or West Lafayette. This postcard was mailed from West Lafayette.

This early postcard shows three people in a canoe on the Wabash River. E.C. Kropp Company of Milwaukee, Wisconsin, published the postcard. People still enjoy canoe rides on the river. It is not deep enough for large boats, but it does have a tendency to flood during spring rains and at other times.

Two

PURDUE UNIVERSITY AND WEST LAFAYETTE

Tecumseh's Trail ran along the Wabash River, which divides Lafayette and West Lafayette. This postcard from the early 1900s was postmarked from West Lafayette in 1912 and mailed to someone in Morristown, New Jersey. The trail led from Battle Ground to the Indiana Soldier's Home along the north side of the Wabash River.

Tecumseh's Trail had walking bridges like this one to cross over streams. Tecumseh Trail Park was a favorite recreation spot at the beginning of the 20th century, but the pavilion, arcade, and other buildings burned to the ground in a 1919 fire, ending the facility. This postcard was mailed in 1910.

Tecumseh's Trail ran along the north side of the Wabash River from Prophet's Town toward what now is West Lafayette. The trail has since disappeared. A historical marker has been put along the river below the Indiana Veterans' Home that says the trail was used by Chief Tecumseh and his warriors before he was defeated at the Battle of Tippecanoe on November 7, 1811.

The Cedar Crest Highway Hotel was on the north edge of West Lafayette near Purdue University on the US 52 Bypass. The postcard above comes from the late 1950s or early 1960s and was produced by Curteichcolor. The postcard says the hotel offered radiant heat, air conditioning, and television. The hotel also had a dining room for its patrons and was open all year from 7:00 a.m. until 8:00 p.m. every day. The hotel is also represented in the drawing below by the Photograph Art Commercial Studio in Lafayette.

In 1937, radio station W9UYM existed in West Lafayette. The call letters indicate that this was a licensed amateur station—regular radio stations have either three or four letters with no numbers. The city of West Lafayette presently has only one radio station. Purdue University has one as well, but it is located in Lafayette.

The Morris Bryant Inn was a popular place in the 1960s, when this postcard was produced. It was on US 52 in West Lafayette, just five minutes from the Purdue University campus. A fire destroyed the motel on April 23, 1994. The owners rebuilt, but it was destroyed again on the grand reopening day by a tornado. The owners decided then not to rebuild.

Arth Drugs, which was part of Rexall, was on Allen Street near Purdue University. This card was published by Harvey's Studio, probably in the 1960s. Rexall drugstores have since declined because of chain drugstores like CVS and Walgreens. The "Rex" in the name came from the common Rx abbreviation for drug prescriptions.

This was the West Lafayette High School until 1939, when a new building was constructed of cream brick and glass at a cost of $225,000. This postcard was mailed in 1909 to someone in North Manchester, Indiana. The school's teams are known as the Red Devils, and their colors are scarlet and gray.

The TraveLodge was located at 200 Brown Street in West Lafayette in the 1950s, when telephone exchanges were still available. The motel changed ownership and became known as the Campus Inn. It is three blocks from the Purdue University campus and three blocks from downtown Lafayette.

The Campus Inn is about a half-mile from the Purdue campus at the intersection of Indiana 231 and US 52. This postcard photograph was taken by Gil Hutton and published by the Photograph Art Commercial Studio, probably in the 1970s. At the time, the Campus Inn was a Best Western motel.

This postcard identifies this motel as the Kings Crown Inn on West Bypass US 52. The motel has since changed hands and is now called the Prestige Inn on Sagamore Parkway West. It is only two minutes from Purdue University. This card was published in the 1950s, when telephone exchange names were still in use.

The Rose Haven Diner used to be on US 52 at the intersection of State Road 28, sixteen miles south of Lafayette. People would stop there on their way to Lafayette or a Purdue University game. Seating capacity was 150. Adjacent to the diner was the Rose Haven Motor Hotel. The diner is no longer in use. (Courtesy of Premier Advertising Company.)

The Gate Entrance at Purdue University was created more than a century ago, and it is still there today. The card identifies it as being in La Fayette, but the university is actually in West Lafayette. The university was founded in 1869 by Lafayette businessman John Purdue. The first classes were held on September 16, 1874.

This postcard was mailed in 1907 and shows Fowler Hall at Purdue University. In 1901, Eliza Fowler made a gift of $70,000 to the university to build the first assembly hall on campus.

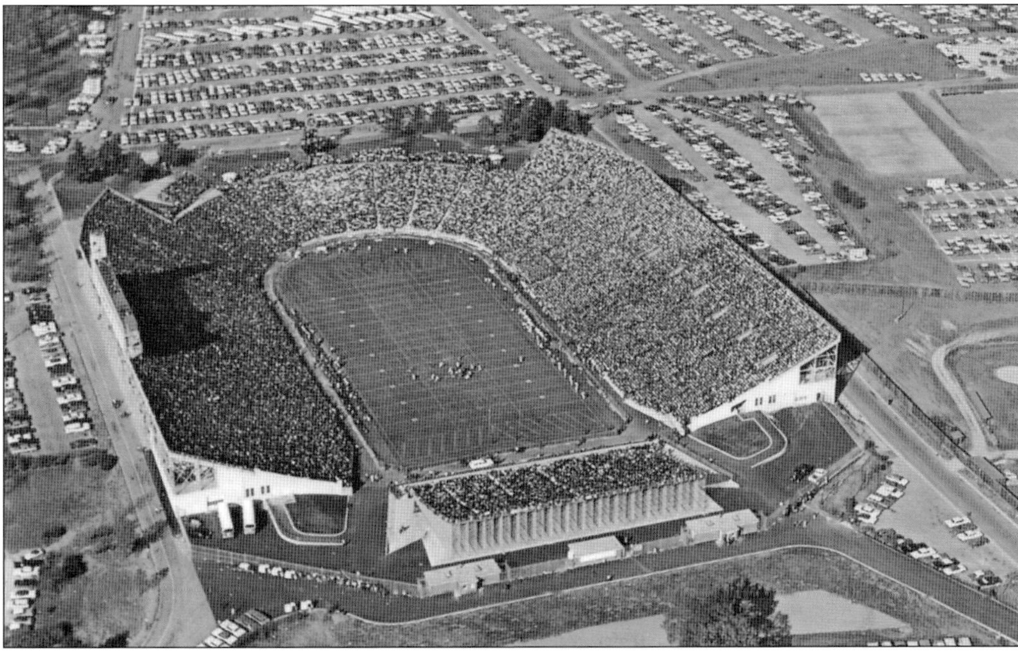

Ross-Ade Stadium opened in 1924. The following year, the Old Oaken Bucket football trophy was introduced and went to the winner of the annual Purdue-Indiana game. The stadium sat 60,200 fans when this postcard was produced around the 1960s by Harvey's Studio. Purdue defeated the USC Trojans by a score of 14-13 in Purdue's first Rose Bowl appearance in 1967.

In four scenes of the Union Club at Purdue University, this postcard shows what the interior decor of the rooms was like in the 1960s. The postcard says that there were 250 overnight guest rooms and that it had fine dining in the Sagamore Room. (Courtesy of ©Penrod/Hiawatha.)

Ground-breaking for the Memorial Union Building by the architectural firm of Irving and Allen Pond of Chicago took place on June 13, 1922. The partially completed building opened on September 9, 1924; it was completed in 1929. This postcard by the Kaplan News Agency was probably the first one of this building.

This was the main lobby for the Memorial Union Building around the 1950s, as published by MacLean Photograph Service. At that time, the Memorial Union had a library for browsing and a recorded music room. A lounge contained a piano for anyone wishing to play. It also had a television.

This postcard shows the Purdue Memorial Union Building about 50 years ago. This photograph was taken by D.G. MacLean.

This postcard shows one of the 256 rooms in the Union Club of the Purdue Memorial Union Building in the 1950s. Only 150 rooms were air conditioned and contained a television for guests. There were 90 rooms in the connecting Graduate House. The writer of the card gave the room a D-plus or C-minus rating.

The first library for Purdue University was housed in this building, constructed in 1878. The library occupied the first floor and a mezzanine, while other classrooms and offices occupied the upper floors. The library moved from this location in 1913. The building became University Hall and now houses the history department.

This postcard shows the Livestock Judging Pavilion at Purdue University. The Indiana 4-H livestock judging program began in April 1919 at the first 4-H Club Round-Up at Purdue University. Livestock judging teams still compete at Purdue to enhance the development and marketable skills of students. The Department of Animal Sciences conducts the program.

The first Heavilon Hall building was constructed in the late 1800s, dedicated on January 19, 1894, and completed in December 1895. It was the home of Purdue University engineering. By 1956, weather and time had taken their toll on the structure, so it was demolished and replaced by another building bearing the same name. The card above was printed in color. Below is another postcard of Heavilon Hall, identified at the "Engineering Building." The black-and-white postcard was mailed to someone in Belmont, Maine, in 1908 from Thorndike. The illustration came from the Post Card Company in New York.

This postcard was produced from a c. 1940s photograph of the Chemical and Metallurgical Engineering Building at Purdue University. The building was constructed in 1940. John L. Bray was the founder of the metallurgy program. The postcard was produced by the Harry Kaplan News Agency.

The Krannert Graduate School of Industrial Administration was built with gifts and grants from Herman C. and Ellnora D. Krannert of Indianapolis. When completed in 1965, it was the tallest academic building on the campus. It incorporated classrooms, libraries, faculty offices, a computer center, and a human behavior laboratory. This card was published by Harvey's Studio.

The Electrical Engineering Building originally had electrical towers on the roof, as seen in this postcard. The towers have since been removed and computer engineering has been added to the building. This postcard was mailed in 1950.

This postcard shows the Gable Courts residence units at the top. On the lower left is a lounge in one of the residence units. At lower right is one of the dining rooms in the Oliver Perkins Terry Memorial House. This postcard was published by the MacLean Photograph Service.

Cary Hall was made possible by a donation from the Cary family in 1927. Franklin Masten Cary and his wife, Jessie Levering, donated $50,000 in 1927 to build Franklin Levering Cary Hall in honor of their son, who died at age 18 just before he was to attend Purdue University.

This postcard from the 1950s shows Cary Hall from the street. Other buildings have been added since this postcard, and now the area is called the Cary Quadrangle, which is the largest residence hall on the Purdue campus and one of the largest halls in the country.

At the entrance to the Men's Quadrangle is Spitzer Court. In the early 1960s, when this postcard was produced, the quadrangle was a complex of five Franklin/Levering Cary Halls and housed about 1,900 undergraduate students. The postcard was mailed in 1962. The photograph was taken by Harold Harvey.

Smith Hall was a gift of the late W.C. Smith of Williamsport. It originally housed the commercial creamery and dairy department at Purdue University. It contains classrooms and laboratories as well as offices for members of the dairy staff. It now has a butcher shop that is open twice weekly. This postcard was produced by the Harry Kaplan News Agency.

Mackey Arena was called Purdue Arena when it opened in 1967. The name was changed in 1972 in honor of long-time athletic director Guy "Red" Mackey. This postcard from the American Marketing Associates, which is no longer in existence, says the arena had a capacity of 14,123. This has since been increased to 14,846.

Stanley Coulter Hall was dedicated on May 17, 1917, as the biology building. It was named after a man who joined the faculty in 1887 and became the first dean of the School of Science in 1907 and the first dean of men in 1919. Today, the hall is the home to the School of Languages and Cultures.

This postcard shows the mall area of Purdue University. The mall gives the campus some green space, something lacking in other areas of the crowded university, which now has many buildings on its 2,602 acres in West Lafayette. This postcard shows just a few blocks of the sprawling campus. (Courtesy of ©Penrod/Hiawatha.)

This postcard shows a view of Purdue University from probably around 1918. Heavilon Hall is in the background, but from what building this photograph was taken is unknown. The postcard was made in Germany and published by the Indiana News Company.

This postcard captures the Purdue campus in the early 1900s. Heavilon Hall is on the right. In the middle is a large smokestack, which has since been torn down. The building on the left is Fowler Hall; behind it is the Engineering Building. This postcard was mailed in 1910.

Fountain at Purdue University, La Fayette, Ind.

This postcard shows a water fountain that was on the campus in the early 1900s. The building on the right is the Engineering Building. The large smokestack next to it has since been replaced by a clock tower. The postcard was mailed in 1909 to someone in Oxford, Indiana.

Somebody wrote on the front of this card that the Civil Building was one of the new buildings on the Purdue campus on November 26, 1907. This building was completed in 1906 for the School of Civil Engineering. The second and larger portion of the building was completed in 1927.

This was originally the Boarding Hall, completed in 1874. It contained the university's primary dining room as well as the living quarters for Purdue's faculty and their families. It later became Ladies Hall for female students. It was demolished in 1927.

Wood Hall is a residence hall for women and was named after Elizabeth G. and William R. Wood. The hall is still in use today. This postcard is from about the 1940s, based on the vehicles parked at the hall. It was produced by the Harry Kaplan News Agency.

This photograph by John Penrod shows the Slayter Center of the Performing Arts, an outdoor entertainment center named for Dr. Games Slayter, the inventor of fiberglass, and his wife, Marie. The concert band shell was completed in 1964 and dedicated on May 1, 1965. The theater can hold up to 20,000 people. (Courtesy of ©Penrod/Hiawatha.)

The Home Economics Building was opened in 1923 and later was known as Home Economics II when the building now known as Stone Hall was completed in 1954. It was renamed in 1976 to the Meredith Residence Hall in honor of Virginia Claypool Meredith, who founded the Department of Home Economics at Purdue in 1905. She was known as the "Queen of American Agriculture." She was raised on a farm in Connersville, Indiana, and became the head of her husband's family farm near Cambridge City. Below is what Virginia C. Meredith Hall looks like today. It houses more than 600 women.

This postcard shows the Purdue Field House, later renamed Lambert Fieldhouse in honor of longtime basketball coach Ward "Piggy" Lambert. It was built in 1937 by David Ross and George Ade as a replacement to the Memorial Gymnasium. The Purdue basketball team used it until Mackey Arena was built next door in 1967.

Here is an inside view of the old Purdue Field House before it was renamed in honor of the coach. It had a concrete foundation; the basketball floor was removed after the season and stored until the next season. Lambert Fieldhouse seated 8,500 people. The Harry Kaplan News Agency published this postcard.

This was the first Memorial Gymnasium, constructed in 1909 in memory of 17 Purdue University football players, coaches, alumni, and fans who perished in a railroad accident on October 31, 1903. It was renovated in 1985 to house the computer science department and renamed Felix Haas Hall. This card was mailed in 1910.

The Pharmacy Building at Purdue University opened its doors in 1930. The two-year School of Pharmacy was founded at Purdue in 1884. In 1985, the school moved into the new Robert E. Heine Pharmacy Building. The school is now known as the College of Pharmacy.

The Hall of Music was dedicated on May 3–4, 1940. In 1958, Purdue immortalized the man who had the vision to create the majestic concert hall by renaming it the Edward C. Elliott Hall of Music. It is connected to the administration building, now called Hovde Hall after a former president of the university. The postcard below shows what the administration building first looked like.

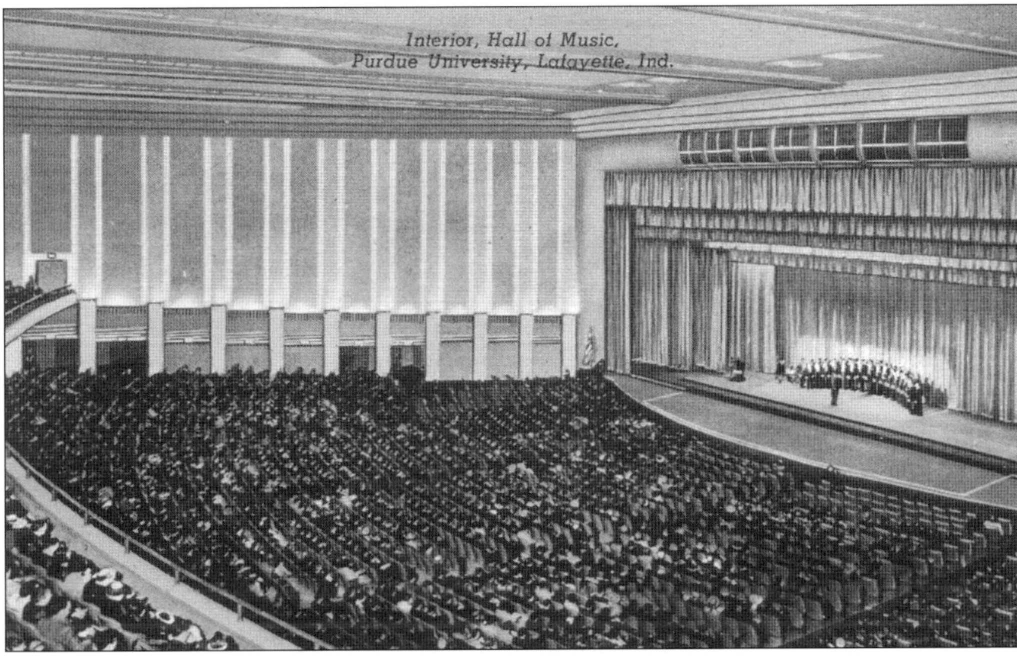

This was the interior of the Hall of Music when it was built in 1940. Seating 6,208 people, it was the largest structure of its kind in America when completed. It is still in use today for concerts, broadway musicals, operas, ballets, symphonies, lecturers, and comedians.

The agricultural department buildings are in the foreground of this postcard. This aerial photograph was probably taken in the 1960s and shows how large Purdue University was at the time. It has grown even more since then. This postcard was published by Harvey's Studio and printed by Dexter Press.

This postcard shows the Agricultural Experiment Station at Purdue. The agricultural department was established in 1903, and this building was constructed soon after that. Alfred Wiancko became the first head of the department in the Agricultural Experiment Station. The Harry Kaplan News Agency published this postcard in the early 1900s.

Agriculture Hall was built in 1901 and was given a $14-million renovation in 2003. It was renamed the David C. Pfendler Hall of Agriculture in 2001 in honor of the esteemed counselor and administrator who spent 35 years at Purdue University. This card was printed by the Fort Wayne Printing Company.

This was the old Poultry Building at Purdue University. The building has since been replaced by a modern facility. Purdue is one of the world's leading colleges of agriculture, food, life, and natural resource sciences. This postcard was produced by the Wayne Novelty and Publishing Company in Fort Wayne.

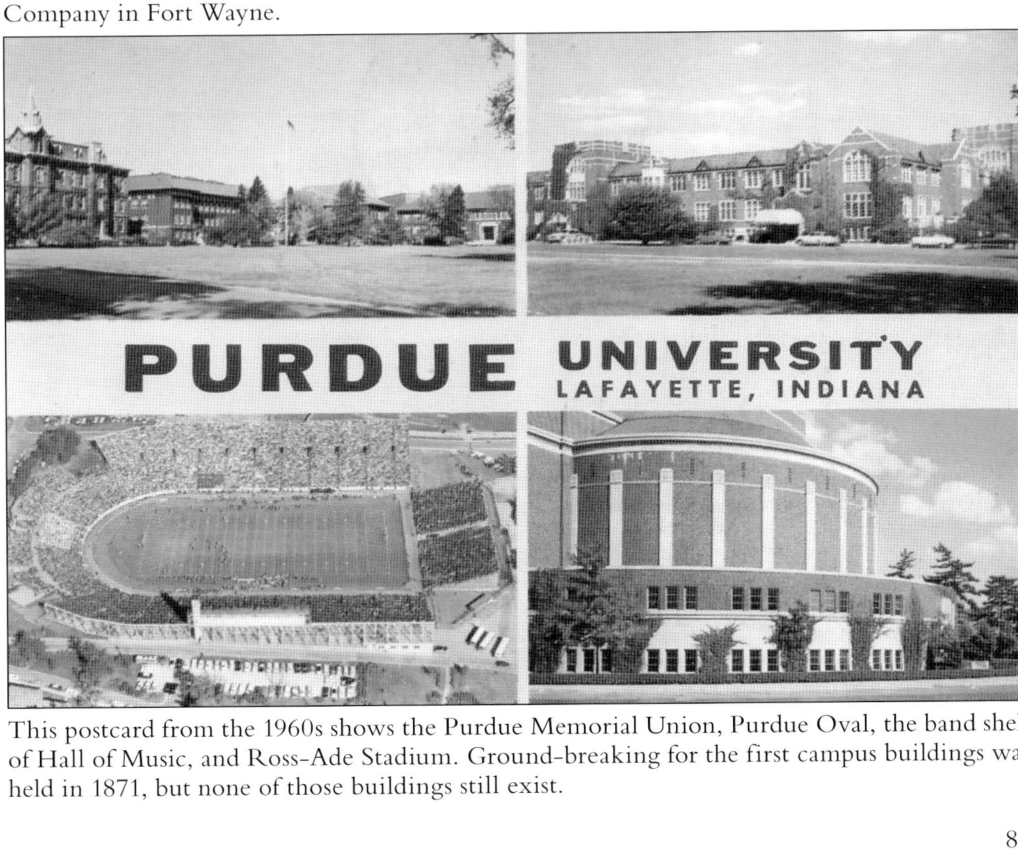

This postcard from the 1960s shows the Purdue Memorial Union, Purdue Oval, the band shell of Hall of Music, and Ross-Ade Stadium. Ground-breaking for the first campus buildings was held in 1871, but none of those buildings still exist.

The Purdue University All-American Marching Band spells out the name of the university at a football game at Ross-Ade Stadium in the 1970s. The card claims the band was the largest university band in the country. The stadium opened on November 22, 1924, with a seating capacity of 13,500. The Purdue band was first formed in 1886. This card was mailed in 1977.

University Presbyterian Church began holding services for Purdue University students in 1939. This postcard was probably first published around 1960. In 2014, Purdue purchased the building for $2.4 million. Next to the church is the Westminster Foundation at Purdue. This postcard was published by MacLean Photograph Service in Decatur, Indiana.

The University Lutheran Chapel Student Center was first organized in 1945 to provide Lutheran services to Purdue University students and was sponsored by the St. James Lutheran Church. The church was built in 1951 and is affiliated with the Lutheran Church Missouri Synod. It is located on Northwestern Avenue. This card was distributed by the Twin City News Agency in Lafayette.

The Boilermaker Special was first presented to the student body at a convocation ceremony in 1940. The Special, a locomotive mounted on an automobile chassis, appears at many events in the area to promote the university.

This "Greetings" postcard shows the Women's Residence Hall, Executive Building, Chemistry Building interior, Hall of Music, University Hall, Recitation Building, Home Economics Building, Hall of Music, University Library, Eliza Fowler Hall, Cary Hall, Men's Residence, and Field House. It was mailed in 1956 to someone in Allentown, Pennsylvania.

The Chemistry Building at Purdue University was constructed in 1907. This was the first building solely occupied by the department. It became overcrowded in 1927 while trying to serve 2,000 students enrolled in chemistry classes. To help alleviate these conditions, another building was constructed. Chemistry was one of the first courses offered by the university when it opened its doors in 1874.

This is one of several buildings for graduate student housing at Purdue University. This one provided 505 rooms for 739 graduate students and conference guests. Purdue has more apartments on and off campus for graduates. This postcard was published by Harvey's Studio of Valparaiso.

Loeb Memorial Fountain was completed in 1959. It was located on the mall in front of the Executive Building at Purdue University. It was a gift of the Bert E. and June Loeb Foundation in memory of Solomon Loeb, who owned Loeb's department store in Lafayette. The fountain was placed in storage in 1988 and reinstalled in Founders Park in 1993.

The Purdue Memorial Center supplements student, faculty, and conference facilities for the adjacent Purdue Memorial Union. This is the west view of the facility. This postcard was produced by MacLean Photograph Service in Decatur, Indiana. Below is another view of the Purdue Memorial Center. At the time, it housed 850,000 volumes in its library and had an audio visual center.

This postcard shows the main foyer of the Purdue Memorial Center. To the left are the library reading rooms and lounges. Entrance to the 1,052-seat Loeb Playhouse is at the rear. This postcard was mailed in 1962. It was published by MacLean Photograph Service.

This Purdue Memorial Center relief is a large limestone carving that depicts man's advancement through life. It was carved by sculptor G.J. Busche. Part of the relief shows a man graduating from college. The postcard comes from Harvey's Studio in Lebanon, Indiana.

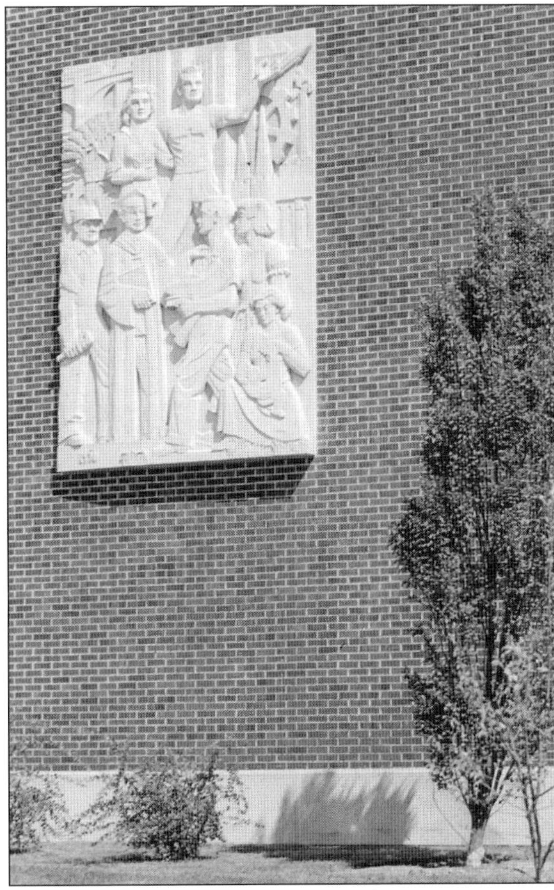

This postcard shows the oldest section of the Purdue University campus, the historic Oval, in the 1950s. The buildings in the photograph are University Hall, Recitation Building, Biology Annex, and Stanley Coulter Hall. Founder John Purdue is buried at the foot of the flagpole. The postcard was mailed in 1960. Someone wrote "German" above one of the buildings because she was studying it there.

This 1920s postcard shows the Kappa Kappa Gamma sorority at Purdue University. The sorority was founded in 1870, and the Gamma Delta Chapter at Purdue was founded on January 24, 1919. As of June 2016, the chapter had initiated 2,715 women.

The Purdue University Recreational Gymnasium opened in 1957 and was built at a cost of $2.5 million. It included this Olympic-sized outdoor pool, which is enjoyed by students and staff and their guests. This postcard was produced by Harvey's Studio in Valparaiso.

This aerial view of Purdue University captures Women's Residence Hall (the X-shaped building), State Street Courts, and Harrison Courts. On the right is the recreational gymnasium with its outdoor pool. The photograph was taken by Harold Harvey and published by Dexter Press around 1960.

The World's Largest Drum

The Purdue All-American Marching Band boasts the World's Largest Drum during its performances for the Boilermakers football team. The band was first established in 1886 and has become an icon of the university, performing in China, Ireland, and Colombia. (Courtesy of ©Penrod/Hiawatha.)

This aerial photograph from the turn of the 21st century shows just how large Purdue University has grown since it first began in 1874 with a couple of structures. Now it encompasses some

2,602 acres to handle a student population of more than 40,000. It has the second largest student population in the state. (Courtesy of ©Penrod/Hiawatha.)

The Maurice G. Knoy Hall of Technology is home for the School of Technology. Knoy was the president of the board of trustees from 1968 to 1979. Construction started in 1982 and was completed in 1984. It was the first campus building to use solar power in 2000. This photograph was taken by John Penrod. (Courtesy of ©Penrod/Hiawatha.)

This aerial photograph of Purdue University shows some of the athletic fields and the athletic department. The card shows the soccer fields, baseball diamond, and track and field stadium used by the university. The card was published by the Harry Kaplan News Agency.

PURDUE'S GOLDEN GIRL

Valeria Ludwick was Purdue's Golden Girl XIII, 1983–1987. The 26-year-old native of Richland, Washington, was a five-time grand national twirling champion and graduate student at Purdue who was working on a doctorate in sports psychology. The Golden Girl first came on the scene at the university in 1954. (Courtesy of ©Penrod/Hiawatha.)

An unidentified Golden Girl is seen in this postcard. The world-famous baton twirler appears with the Purdue University All-American Marching Band whenever it performs. This postcard was made by Dexter Press in West Nyack, New York. (Courtesy of ©Penrod/Hiawatha.)

Purdue Pete is a mascot of Purdue University, first designed as a logo by the university bookstore in 1940. The bookstore would put the mascot on its products and portray him dressed up in different clothes for different majors. He was given a physical identity in 1956 as he came out and helped the students cheer at a pep rally. This postcard was mailed in 1961.

Stone Lions Fountain was dedicated in 1904 and was a gift of the class of 1903. It quit operating in the 1920s or 1930s. On April 22, 2001, it was rededicated and again started serving as a water fountain. It sits at the southeast corner of Stanley Coulter Hall, which was its original location. This postcard was mailed in 1908.

The Horticulture Garden at Purdue offers beautiful flowers and plants. The garden was first established in 1982. It is on Marstellar Street adjacent to the Horticulture Building. The garden is home to hundreds of annual and perennial flowers and foliage plants. The tree peony collection is noteworthy.

Purdue University has had three armory buildings in its history. The first burned down in 1918 and was rebuilt that year. The second building suffered a fire on January 13, 1928; it did not burn down, but it had to be rebuilt. The armory was rebuilt once more, and the 1928 building still stands.

The WRH crest still exists today in front of the Windsor Halls complex, the oldest women's residence halls on the Purdue University campus. The complex comprises five distinct buildings—Duhme, Shealy, Vawter, Warren, and Wood. The crest represents protection.

Three

Fort Ouiatenon

This postcard was likely produced soon after the replica blockhouse of Fort Ouiatenon was built in 1930. The back of the card gives the history of the original fort: it was erected in 1717 by the French; became English in 1763 and American in 1779; and was destroyed in 1791.

A British guard reenactor stands by the replica blockhouse of Fort Ouiatenon, which was built in 1930 by Richard Wetherill, a local physician. The replica is now the focal point of a county park. The true site of the fort was discovered in the late 1960s. The British held the fort from 1763 until 1779.

This replica blockhouse of Fort Ouiatenon and a shed are much smaller than the original fort that was established by the French some miles away. The fort served as a trading post and stopping point for the voyageurs from Quebec. This postcard was mailed from Lafayette to someone in LaPorte, Indiana, in 1952 for 2¢.

This postcard shows a reenactor in the gift shop in the reconstructed blockhouse in the Fort Ouiatenon Museum. The trader offers replicas of 18th-century French and Indian trade items for sale. This postcard was made by Dexter Press, and the photograph was taken by Photography Associates in Monticello, Indiana.

Reenactors dress in costumes depicting life at 18th-century Fort Ouiatenon during the annual Feast of the Hunter's Moon in late September and early October. Reenactors dress as frontiersmen, Indians, and soldiers during the feast. The blockhouse is located next to a park on South River Road in West Lafayette.

The firing of the cannons is one of the highlights of the Feast of the Hunter's Moon. The annual event is held at Fort Ouiatenon on the banks of the Wabash River. Reenactors representing the British "battle" reenactors representing the French during the festival. Visitors enjoy an array of handcrafted items and taste-tempting foods. (Courtesy of ©Penrod/Hiawatha.)

This postcard shows a mural by Edward Blackwell depicting a council at Fort Ouiatenon in 1765. Peace terms were conceded by Chief Pontiac to England's king, represented by George Crogan, an Indian trader and deputy superintendent for Indian affairs, concluding the French and Indian War. (Courtesy of ©Penrod/Hiawatha.)

Fort Ouiatenon Information Center, Lafayette, Indiana

This postcard of the interior of the French colonial frontier fur trading post at Fort Ouiatenon shows the gift shop. The gift shop offers authentic reproductions of French and British 18th-century trade items. This postcard was published by Harvey's Studio in Valparaiso.

Four

Indiana State Soldiers' Home

When the Indiana State Soldiers' Home was built in the late 1800s, the front entrance looked like this. This postcard was made in Germany and never mailed. The old cannon at the gate probably came from the Civil War; it is gone, but the rest of the gate remains the same. The road now goes to the right of the pillar at right.

The front entrance to the Indiana Veterans' Home still looks like this postcard, which was probably produced in the late 1940s by Harvey's Studio in Valparaiso. However, "Visitors Welcome" has been replaced by "Indiana Veterans' Home" on the sign. The entrance is on Indiana State Road 43, which leads to downtown West Lafayette to the south and Battle Ground to the north.

The grounds at the Indiana Veterans' Home are well kept and beautiful, as seen in this postcard of a fountain and two circular gardens on the circle. The Kaplan News Agency produced this card before 1952, when the rate went up from 1¢ to 2¢ on January 1.

This is a postcard of the road that snakes it way up the hill from Indiana 43 to the Indiana State Soldiers' Home. The road has gone through some improvements over the years; it is now smooth sailing up the high hill. This card was mailed in 1907.

This postcard, mislabelled as the administration building at the Indiana Soldiers' Home, actually shows the commandant's residence. It was one of the first buildings constructed at the site, which occupied 242 acres of land that was once a forest. This building still stands today, but many others have long since been demolished.

The commandant's residence was completed in September 1899. The building in the background was the administrative building and is no longer in use. It had rooms for the board of directors to use while they attended monthly meetings. It is undergoing restorations.

This scene at the Indiana State Soldiers' Home was photographed by the Wabash River. Retired Army general Richard P. DeHart gifted 1,900 feet of riverfront property to the home. The land there is known as the Tecumseh Trails Park. This postcard was probably produced in the 1940s by the Harry Kaplan News Agency.

This is how the parade grounds looked at the Indiana State Soldiers' Home in the early 1900s. This card mistakenly places the home in La Fayette. It was mailed in 1915. In the background is what was called the Old Men's Building, which has since been replaced with a modern structure.

This postcard shows two buildings at the Indiana State Soldiers' Home, the chapel and the Old Men's Building. These two buildings were not part of the original construction in 1895. They were built in 1897, after the state appropriated $61,723.61 for their construction in addition to other improvements. Neither building exists today.

This postcard identifies this building as the new hospital at the Indiana State Soldiers' Home. The hospital was one of the first buildings constructed in 1895, and opened for business on February 1 the following year. The card was mailed in 1917. The building has since been replaced by a modern structure.

This postcard shows the Old People's Building at the Indiana State Soldiers' Home. It was occupied by old soldiers and their wives who were too feeble to walk to the main dining room for meals. The tower was 148 feet high and could be seen for miles. It has since been torn down. This postcard was mailed in 1917.

This postcard of the Indiana State Soldiers' Home shows the parade ground of the facility. The card was published by O.L. Foster, a commercial photographer in Lafayette. It only had a small writing space on the photograph side of the card. None of the buildings pictured exist today.

The library was one of the first buildings constructed at the Indiana State Soldiers' Home. It was later named the Lawrie Library in honor of Capt. Alexander Lawrie, who painted more than 160 portraits of Union officers from the Civil War. The library still exists today but is no longer in use and has a sign that reads "Asbestos Hazard."

Members and guests enjoy a parade at the Indiana Veterans' Home. This card was produced by the Artvue Post Card Company of New York.

The Indiana Veterans' Home sits on a hill up from the Wabash River, so these steps were built to allow people to walk down to the river from the home. People could then walk along Tecumseh's Trail alongside the river; however, that trail has since disappeared, as have the steps.

Five

Battle Ground

This gate marks the entrance to the Tippecanoe Battlefield in Battle Ground. The battlefield was named a national historic landmark on October 9, 1960. It is now maintained by the Tippecanoe County Historical Association. This postcard was mailed in 1929 to someone in Evansville, Indiana.

The postcard above mistakenly identifies the Soldier's Monument as being in Lafayette; it is actually in nearby Battle Ground. The 80-foot obelisk memorial was built in 1908 and commemorates 63 Americans who died in the Battle of Tippecanoe on November 7, 1811. The card was mailed in 1911. The postcard at left properly places the monument in Battle Ground. It says the battle was fought by Gen. William Henry Harrison—perhaps it should have said "led by" instead. Harrison later became the ninth president of the United States, but only served a month.

The Tippecanoe Battlefield in Battle Ground is a stone's throw north of West Lafayette. This postcard incorrectly identifies it as being in Lafayette. A monument was built there in 1908, and a large commemoration of the 150th anniversary was held in 1961. An amphitheater was added to the memorial in 1986. This card was mailed in 1912.

The Tippecanoe Historical Association maintains a bookstore in Carpenter Hall, located in Battle Ground across from the battlefield. The building is also used for discussion groups, recreation, classes, and general meetings. It is part of the Battle Ground Methodist Camp, Northwest Indiana Conference. This postcard was published by Harvey's Studio.

The Battle Ground Methodist Camp is across from where the famous Battle of Tippecanoe was fought. The retreat center contains complete facilities for housing, feeding, and programming for 40 people. This building was the beginning of a modernization program started in 1960. The card was published in 1978 by Harvey's Studio.

The photograph on this postcard is of Prophet's Rock in Battle Ground. The Prophet, who was the brother of Shawnee chief Tecumseh, shouted incantations for the success of his warriors. He told them the bullets the white man fired at them would be harmless. The card was published by the Adolph Selige Publishing Company of St. Louis.

Bibliography

American Football Database. "Boilermaker Special." americanfootballdatabase.wikia.com/wiki/Boilermaker_Special.

Asylum Projects. "Wabash Sanitarium." www.asylumprojects.org/index.php/Wabash_Sanitarium.

Bangert, David. "Purdue Buys University Church; Congregation has to Move." *Indianapolis Star*, April 13, 2014.

Central Presbyterian Church. "History of Our Church." www.centralpreschurch.org/history-of-our-church.

"FBI Probes Pay Phone Near Courthouse." *Chicago Tribune*, August 10, 1998.

First Baptist Church of Lafayette. "Who We Have Been." firstbaptistlafayette.org/sample-page/who-we-have-been.

Girl Scouts of Central Indiana. "Camp Sycamore Valley." www.girlscoutsindiana.org.

Guyer, Danielle. "Preservations Efforts Hailed." *Agricultures Magazine*, winter 2002.

History of Purdue University Mascots. "The History of Purdue Pete." purduemascots.weebly.com/petes-origins.html.

"Indiana Flood of 1913 Remembered." *USA Today*, March 24, 2015.

Indiana Veterans' Home. "A Brief History of IVH." in.gov/ivh/2367.htm.

Kappa Kappa Gamma Delta Chapter. "Chapter History." purdue.kappa.org/chapter-history

Kriebel, Robert C. *Old Lafayette Volume II, 1854–1876*. Tippecanoe County Historical Assoc., 1990.

Lafayette Country Club. "History." www.lafayettecountryclub.net/history.

Lyles School of Civil Engineering. "A History of the School of Engineering." eng.purdue.edu/jump/c137fa.

Purdue Science Department of Chemistry. "Purdue Chemistry – A Brief History." www.chem.purdue.edu/about_us/history.php.

Purdue Sports. "Lambert Fieldhouse." www.purduesports.com/facilities/lambert-fieldhouse.html.

Purdue Today. "Did you know? Ladies Hall." March 5, 2015. www.purdue.edu/newsroom/purduetoday/didyouknow/2015/Q1/did-you-know-ladies-hall.html.

———. "Did you know? Loeb Fountain." August 16, 2013. www.purdue.edu/newsroom/purduetoday/didyouknow/2013/Q3/did-you-know-loeb-fountain.html.

———. "Did you know? Stone Lions Fountain." January 30, 2015. www.purdue.edu/newsroom/purduetoday/didyouknow/2015/Q1/did-you-know-stone-lions-fountain.html.

Purdue University. "Purdue History." www.purdue.edu/purdue/about/history.html.

Purdue University Army ROTC. "Purdue University Army ROTC History." polytechnic.purdue.edu/armyrotc/overview/history.

Purdue University College of Liberal Arts. "Heavilon Hall." www.cla.purdue.edu/resources/buildings/heavilon.html.

———. "Stanley Coulter Hall." www.cla.purdue.edu/resources/buildings/stanley.html.

———. "University Hall." https://www.cla.purdue.edu/resources/buildings/university.html.

Purdue University Department of Computer Science. "Memorial Gymnasium Named after Prof. Haas." www.cs.purdue.edu/news/articles/2006/haas-gymnasium.html.

Purdue University Division of Recreational Sports. "Building History." web.ics.purdue.edu/~bxd/recsports.html.

Purdue University Hall of Music Productions. "Venues – Eliza Fowler Hall." www.purdue.edu/hallofmusic/Venues/Fowler/Fowler.html.

———. "Venues – Elliott Hall of Music." www.purdue.edu/hallofmusic/Venues/Eliott/Elliott.html.

———. "Venues – Slayter Center." www.purdue.edu/hallofmusic/Venues/Slayer/Slayter.html.
Purdue University Horticulture. "Purdue Horticulture Gardens." ag.purdue.edu/hla/Hort/Pages/HortGardens.aspx.
Purdue University Purdue Bands & Orchestras. " 'All-American' Marching Band." www.purdue.edu/bands/ensembles/aamb/.
———. "Golden Girls of History." www.purdue.edu/bands/ensembles/auxiliaries/the-golden-girl/history/.
Purdue University Tippecanoe County. "Fort Ouiatenon." www.tippecanoe.in.gov/Facilities/Facility/Details/Fort-Ouiatenon-3.
Purdue University University Residences. "Meredith Hall." www.housing.purdue.edu/Housing/Residences/Meredith/index.html.
———. "Windsor Halls." www.housing.purdue.edu/Housing/Residences/Windsor/index.html.
Smithsonian National Postal Museum. "The 150th Anniversary of the Balloon *Jupiter* Airmail Flight." postalmuseum.si.edu/collections/object-spotlight/balloon-jupiter.html.
Stadium Journey. "Lighting Up the Mackey Arena." stadiumjourney.com/stadium/mackey-arena.
"Then & Now: John T. Myers Pedestrian Bridge, 1993." *Lafayette Journal & Courier*, September 17, 2014.
Visit Lafayette–West Lafayette."Fort Ouiatenon." www.homeofpurdue.com/attractions/fortouiatenon.html.
Woods, Paula and Fern Martin. *Traveling Through Tippecanoe*. St. Louis, MO: G. Bradley Publishing, 1991.

Discover Thousands of Local History Books Featuring Millions of Vintage Images

Arcadia Publishing, the leading local history publisher in the United States, is committed to making history accessible and meaningful through publishing books that celebrate and preserve the heritage of America's people and places.

Find more books like this at
www.arcadiapublishing.com

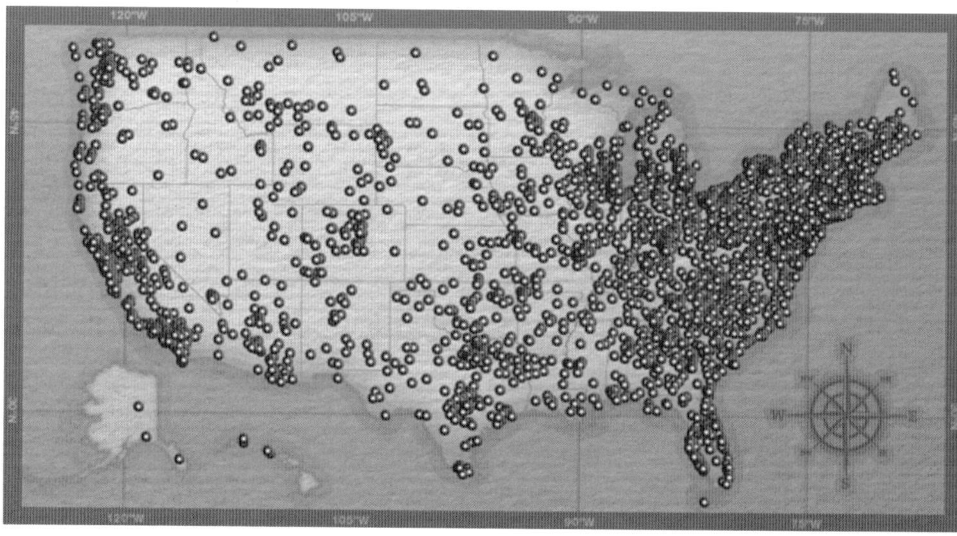

Search for your hometown history, your old stomping grounds, and even your favorite sports team.

Consistent with our mission to preserve history on a local level, this book was printed in South Carolina on American-made paper and manufactured entirely in the United States. Products carrying the accredited Forest Stewardship Council (FSC) label are printed on 100 percent FSC-certified paper.

MADE IN THE USA